IDLE STONES

COMPILED BY
EILEEN WHITE M.A., PH.D.
for the
IDLE AND THACKLEY
HERITAGE GROUP

1997

IN MEMORY OF

Dorothy Lucy **White**
1909-1996
an off comed'un who lived in Idle for 60 years
Secretary of the Idle and Thackley Heritage Group

Francis **Wilfred White**
1902-1997
an Idle man all his life whose long service to Upper Chapel was
recognised by the gift of Maundy money from the Queen
in Bradford Cathedral 27 March 1997

Published by the Idle and Thackley
Heritage Group

© Eileen White M.A., Ph.D., 1997

ISBN 0 9520499 3 7

Designed by John Barrett

Typesetting by
Highlight Type Bureau Ltd., Bradford

Printed by Birch Printers (Bradford) Ltd.

*Front Cover: Junction of Bradford Canal
and the Leeds and Liverpool Canal at
Windhill (Derek Shepherd)*

Introduction

Stone is the essential building material of the Township of Idle, giving character to the old village and hamlets. It was not always utilized, however, and the Survey of Idle in 1584 gave more consideration to the commercial value of the woods, although the potential of wall stones and slates from quarries was acknowledged, along with that of coal mines. At that time, shallow open-cast mining would have been usual. We can imagine most houses to have been built of timber-framing, with thatched roofs. Stone buildings that survive today date from the 17th century, with the Old Chapel at Town Gate and nearby large houses and barns in Westfield Lane, Town Lane and the top of High Street. These probably replaced earlier structures: when Town Well Fold, High Street, was renovated in the early 1970s, medieval timber framing was found embedded in the early 17th century stone shell.

Commercial exploitation had to wait for the development of transport systems. First came the network of canals, which were promoted as a means of bringing together coal, stone and other materials of the Industrial Revolution. With the Leeds to Liverpool Canal and Bradford Canal passing within the Township boundaries, Idle was well placed to benefit from Bradford's expansion and build up its textile and quarrying businesses. Because the getting of stone could now be done at a commercial level, not only the houses of the well-off, but also cottages for the growing number of workers could be built in stone, and a range of examples from the end of the 18th century to the early 20th century survive. These buildings are an extension of the land on which they are built. Development took place on a small scale by local builders, gradually moving out from the original centres, following the pattern of fields and long established roads and trackways. Because the local stone was used, new and old stand side by side in harmony.

In time the quarries were worked out, or ceased to become profitable, and advanced technology and transport enabled the same building materials to be used anywhere in the country. The second half of the 20th century has seen most of the remaining open spaces of Idle given up to housing. Using cement and pebble-dash (Thorpe Edge Estate), red brick (Cote Farm) or (as in the case of the Idle Medical Centre which has been greeted with horror by local residents) reconstituted stone blocks and varnished plywood, these later buildings are in danger of destroying the character of Idle because they can be built identically in any part of the country. It is fortunate that the new houses on Bradford Road near The Green in the centre of Idle were built in the early 1970s of reclaimed stone in a style sensitive to their surroundings. The building material makes all the difference: a few houses at the bottom of Ley Fleaks Road, although part of the same scheme, were constructed in a dreary brown brick before the policy of building to match the old village character was adopted.

Working the stone

When William Cudworth went *Round About Bradford* in 1876, the stone industry was well established, and he reported that the quality of Idle stone meant it was used for public buildings in the large towns of England, and was also exported to the Continent, and as far away as South America, China and Australia. There were many firms of stone merchants, including William Child; Thomas Denbigh; John Sharp of All Alone Quarry; Bottomley & Hill; and Cousens, Thackray & Co. at the beginning of the 19th century. In the second half there were Baxter & Upton; Firth & Padgett; and Nowell & Robson. The largest firm was that of the Vint family. George, Ebenezer Sharp and Samuel were the sons of William Vint, Minister of Upper Chapel in Westfield Lane, who inherited the stone business from their mother's brother John Sharp.

In the 1870s the firm employed between three and four hundred workers, and dominated the activity at Gaisby Quarry and on Idle Moor.

In the area below Five Lane Ends, between Highfield Road and Bradford Road, at Gaisby Quarry, on Westfield Lane and at All Alone, stone was excavated from the ground leaving large holes – up to 90 feet deep at Gaisby – but across Idle Moor it was mined. It would take up to five months to dig a shaft down to a depth of about 44 yards until the seams of stone were reached. Then 5 feet of shale or rag would have to be removed from above the stone, often with the help of explosives, before the block could be cut free, dragged along the tunnels on rails to the shafts, and finally raised to the surface, to be dressed into blocks, wallstones, slates or cobbles. The roofs of the tunnels and places from where the stone was removed were kept up by wooden props or walls built from quarry spoil. Once props were removed, or as a result of underground explosions by other miners, tunnels could collapse. Water had to be continually pumped out of these workings, so once the stone was taken and the pumps removed the cavities would flood. The whole of Idle Moor, from Idle Hill Reservoir to Highfield Road, is riddled with abandoned tunnels. Vints had ten shafts across the Moor, and did not keep a full record of the extent of underground workings that radiated from them. Those people who buy new houses on the Moor cannot be aware of what went on below the surface.

The old stone buildings of Idle, Thackley, Thorp, Windhill and Wrose have a sense of belonging to the ground on which they are built that no brick building can achieve. This book celebrates the achievement of the quarrymen and builders who gave us Idle stones.

The Canal

Bradford businessmen were prominent in the creation of the Leeds and Liverpool Canal, and the branch canal to Bradford was an essential element of the scheme. Topography dictated that this branch should be cut along the one exit from the depression in which Bradford is built, going north to the Aire Valley. Consequently, the Bradford Canal ran on the Wrose and Windhill side of Bradford Beck, and the Leeds and Liverpool Canal took the Aire Valley route to Skipton, again inside the Idle boundary. The Skipton to Thackley section of the Canal and the Bradford Canal were completed in 1774, and the section to Leeds in 1777.

1 **THE LEEDS AND LIVERPOOL CANAL** at Idle.

2   **A TRADITIONAL HORSE-DRAWN BOAT** on the Canal near Rockcliff.

3   **DOBSON LOCKS** near
     Apperley Bridge.

4 **SWING BRIDGE** on the Canal near Bottom Farm. The Midland Railway bridge is on the left, and a steam train is about to go into Thackley Tunnel.

5 **THE CANAL AT BUCK WOOD.**

6   **THE CANAL TAVERN** on the Leeds and Liverpool Canal, now
     demolished. It stood on the north side of the Canal, opposite Thackley
     West Wood, and the punt seen moored near the door was used to ferry
     people across the canal. Eliza Jane Whiteley, wife of one of the last
     licensees of the Tavern, is seen standing outside.

Canal Architecture

*A horse-drawn boat would travel about 22 miles a day. Later, a steam boat could make the journey from Liverpool
and back in six days. Inevitably, taverns were built for the boatmen along the route, and the men were notorious for
spending too long drinking so that they had to hurry the horses along to make up time. The steam men found ways of
sabotaging the machinery so they could have a longer stop. As further relaxation, they played at dominoes and cards.
Not surprisingly, wives in Liverpool would collect the wage packets for their men before the money could be spent
along the canal.*

7   JUNCTION OF THE BRADFORD CANAL AND THE
     LEEDS AND LIVERPOOL CANAL.

The piece of water on the left is the only remaining part of the Bradford Canal, which was closed in 1922 and eventually filled in. The necessity of building a bridge to take the towpath over to join the towpath on the north side of the main canal resulted in this simple yet harmonious structure. The place, with a house and developing mills, became known as Junction.

The Turnpike Road

8   **LEEDS ROAD** at Thackley.

Road construction was being improved in the early years of the 19th century, especially by use of the system of compacted layers devised by John McAdam. Private enterprise created new, more direct links between towns; the outlay was recovered through tolls levied on the users. Royal Assent was given to an Act for Making a Turnpike Road from Shipley to Bramley on 26 May 1826, and shareholders included many notable Idle people. Tolls went up to 9d (old pence) for coaches and carriages, and it cost 5 shillings to take a score of oxen and 1 shilling for a score of sheep. The road was laid out as straight as possible, cutting across former boundaries; in Idle the triangular portions cut off from the main field were called Three Nook Fields. After the usual delays, the Turnpike Road was finished in the early 1830s, appearing on the 1838 Idle Township Map. In 1872 the Shipley to Bramley Turnpike Road was renamed Leeds Road, a more convenient name as houses were being built along it. In 1878 an Act of Parliament allowed for such roads to be maintained jointly by the Local and County Authorities, and they were "dis-turnpiked".

The Railway

The Midland Railway line from Leeds to Shipley was built through Thackley in 1844-6, including the construction of Thackley Tunnel. The village of Idle did not acquire a line until the early 1870s, and inevitably much disruption occurred as the route from Laisterdyke and Eccleshill through Idle and Thackley to Windhill and Shipley was laid down. Goods trains first ran in 1874, and Idle Station, at the bottom of High Street, opened for passenger transport on 15 April 1875, as did the Shipley and Windhill Station. Thackley had to wait until 1878. All these stations were closed to passenger transport in 1931, although goods trains and the occasional excursion train continued to operate along the route. The Laisterdyke to Idle section was closed to all traffic in 1964, and the remaining section to Shipley in 1968. The line itself was taken up in the early 1970s, a hundred years after it had been built.

9 **GOODS TRAIN AT IDLE.** A London Midland & Scottish Railway designed 2-6-0 locomotive passes over the High Street Bridge towards the goods yard at Idle Station.

10 **A B1 CLASS 4-6-0 CROSSING HIGH STREET BRIDGE.** Regular motive power on the Shipley Great Northern Railway branch was provided by GNR and London North Eastern Railway designed locomotives until the line was near to closure.

11 **A "JUBILEE" CLASS 4-6-0 NO. 45565 "VICTORIA" PASSING THE DISUSED PLATFORMS OF IDLE STATION.** These locomotives were designed by Sir William Stanier for the London Midland & Scottish Railway, and were introduced in 1935, coinciding with King George V's Silver Jubilee.

12 **A "CRAB" 2-6-0**, designed for the London Midland & Scottish Railway, begins the climb towards Eccleshill. It is passing the former private siding of the Yorkshire Engineering and Welding Company works. Judging from the crowds and cars on the Idle Cricket Club field to the right, an important match is taking place.

Delvers and Builders

13 and 14   **QUARRY MEN AT IDLE**.

It was a hard and dangerous job to get the stone from the mines under Idle Moor. Teams were made up of specialist workers: those who sunk the shafts, the miners who bared the stone, the wooders who put in props along the tunnels, the getters of the stone who cut it from the ground, and the jennymen who took the severed stone to the shaft bottom. The better stone was sold in large blocks, and the rest dressed into small wallstones, roof slates, and flags and sets for pavements and roads. In the 1870s, Cavendish Road, Springfield and New Street in Idle and Leeds Road in Thackley were amongst the areas rapidly being developed, making use of the local products.

15 **HOUSES UNDER CONSTRUCTION**
on Leeds Road, Thackley.

Churches

16　**THE OLD CHAPEL**, Town Gate.

This Chapel, opened in 1630, replaced an earlier building that was in decay. When new it would have been one of the few stone buildings in Idle, and it formed a natural centre to the village. There was always an independent streak in Idle, and the curate Thomas Smallwood was ejected in 1662 as a non-conformist. The tension between Anglicans, of the established church, and those of the Presbyterian persuasion meant that it was not until 1692 that Idle Chapel was consecrated by the Archbishop of York.

17 **THE OLD CHAPEL.**

18 **INTERIOR OF THE OLD CHAPEL.** After the parish church
was built, the Old Chapel continued in use as a School and Sunday
School until after the Second World War.

19 and 20   **TOWN GATE** and the Old Chapel.

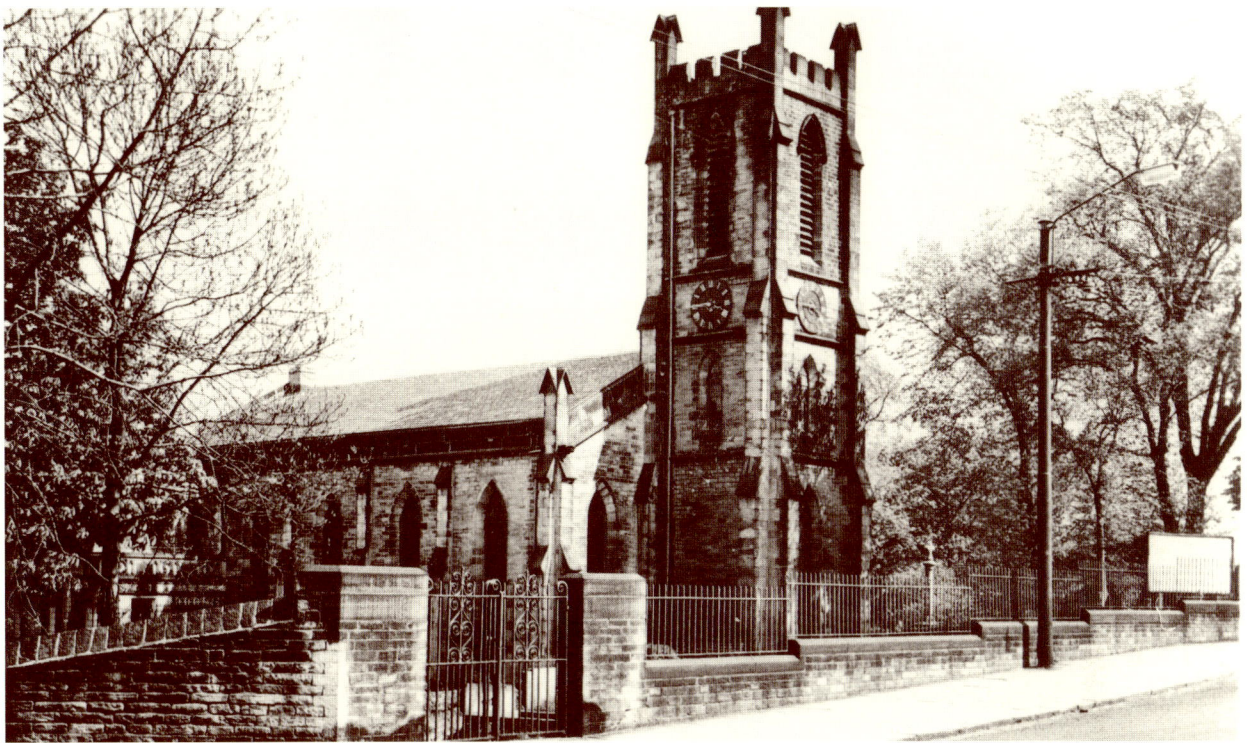

21 **HOLY TRINITY CHURCH**, Idle.

Idle had been part of the parish of Calverley, and the Old Chapel was built as a chapel of ease, so that the villagers did not need to walk to Calverley every week. Growing populations at the beginning of the 19th century made new and larger churches a necessity, and Holy Trinity Church in Idle was built with a donation from the national fund raised in thanksgiving throughout the country after the Battle of Waterloo in 1815. The foundation stone was laid in 1828 and the church was consecrated by the Archbishop of York in 1830.

22 **THE LYCH GATE** at Holy Trinity
commemorates the Idle men who died in the
First and Second World Wars.

23 **INTERIOR OF HOLY TRINITY
CHURCH**, Idle. The west end of the
nave has now been divided off to
create a meeting room.

24 **UPPER CHAPEL**, Westfield Lane, 1850 building.

The side and back of this building reveal the amount of wall stone needed for the 19th century chapels. There were several quarries just above here on Westfield Lane.

The Presbyterians or non-conformists excluded from the Old Chapel eventually acquired land on Westfield Lane and built the Upper Chapel in 1717. This developed into a Congregational Church as it expanded in the 19th century, and a larger chapel was built in 1850 just above the first site. A new organ was installed in 1912, with an extension built at the rear to accommodate it. This may have unsettled the whole structure of the building, which was declared unsafe in 1950. The present church, opened in 1957, stands on the ground of the original chapel.

From small beginnings, other non-conformist denominations began to build their own chapels in Idle.

25 and 26 **THACKLEY METHODIST CHAPEL**, Park Road, 1889.
The first Wesleyan School and Chapel had been opened in
Thackley in 1856, and were damaged by a fire in 1888.

27 and 28   **ST. JOHN'S CHURCH**, Cavendish Road, 1874. This was built as a mission
church of Holy Trinity Parish Church. After a new St. John's was opened on
Thorpe Edge estate in 1963, the Cavendish Road building was demolished.

29   **THE BAPTIST CHURCH**, Bradford Road.

A Baptist church stood on the site from 1810, and this larger building was opened in 1878.
It was demolished in 1983 and the present building also houses a Community Centre, where meetings of the Idle and Thackley Heritage Group meet.

30 **THE UNITARIAN CHAPEL**, Highfield Lane, 1858.
Simpson's Garage incorporates the Sunday School building as a workshop,
but the Chapel itself was demolished.

31 **THE PRIMITIVE METHODIST SUNDAY SCHOOL**, Town Lane,
built in 1882. The adjoining Chapel of 1861 has been demolished, but the
School is now used for youth activities and other community events.

Public Buildings

32   **TOWN LANE** before road widening, 1889.

The Idle Local Board was set up in 1864, with the function of maintaining roads and improving sanitation, water supply and other public amenities. For a short time it met in the old Round Steps School building attached to the Old Chapel, but soon moved to a meeting room in the Oddfellows Hall at the bottom of High Street. It was not until 1888 that the Board acquired Crow Trees House and estate; the house and gardens at front and back were sold to the tenant, and the land along Town Lane was used for a Public Office. Opportunity was taken to widen the road at this point. Trees along the road were sold and cut down in August 1888 and March 1889, a process recorded in this photograph. A similar photograph was said to be illustrating a saw pit, but it is obvious from the records of the Local Board that it was only used for the clearance of trees to widen the road and build the Office.

33 **THE PUBLIC OFFICES**, Town Lane, later Idle Library.

Jowett Kendall, a local architect, designed the Offices in 1888, and the Board took out a loan of £3,960 secured on the General District Rates for 50 years. The building included a meeting room, offices and an attached house to be the residence of the Surveyor, who was in charge of roads and other maintenance in the District. The builders were all local men:

Mason: Albert Cordingley of Thackley.

Plumber: James Padgett of Idle.

Plasterers: Messrs. Hollings & Mitchell of Idle.

Slater: Robert Hartley of Idle.

Joiner: William Barker of Idle.

The Offices were opened on 4 March 1890, and were on public view every evening for the following week.

After Idle was taken into Bradford in 1899, the building was used for a Branch Library from 1901 until 1995, when the Library moved to Albion Road and the Offices were sold to the same Stage School which had bought the Old Chapel.

34 **DECORATIVE PANEL** above the fireplace in the meeting room.

Public Houses

35 **THE SHOULDER OF MUTTON**, Leeds Road, formerly the property of the Ilkley Brewery Company.

36 **THE GREAT NORTHERN**, Leeds Road; its name reflects the railway line behind it, built by the Great Northern Railway Company. Jim Garforth is driving the horse and trap.

Perhaps because quarrying was such thirsty work, there were many public houses in Idle and Thackley, many of which still remain.

37 **THE COMMERCIAL**, Park Road.

Top of Green

38 **BRADFORD ROAD**. The original of this photograph has been
hand coloured by someone who did not know Idle, because the
buildings have been tinted red as if built with brick instead of stone.

*The area to the left in these views was the original village green of Idle,
known as Tithe Laith Green, and this part of Bradford Road was called
"Top of Green". It is interesting to examine the photographs in detail, to
see the gradual changes taking place. Many of the buildings, especially
those at the top, have now been demolished.*

39 and 40   **BRADFORD ROAD**.

41 **GARTH HOUSE** at the top of Thorp Garth, now the site of the Co-op and other shops. It was built at the end of the 18th century.

42 **OLD BARN** at Top of Green near Garth House, in the process of demolition. It had been used by Woodhead's the Butchers as a slaughter house.

The Green

43 and 44 **BOTTOM OF BRADFORD ROAD** near The Green.

The stone cobbles of the road often remain below the modern surface, revealed and further destroyed during successive roadworks. In North Fold and Hampton Place they were relaid after the housing developments.

45   **THE GREEN**, Idle. Keighley's Butchers Shop, on the extreme left, is in a house dating from the 18th century, while the building in front of the railway was put up in 1878, replacing the old Tithe Barn and house.

Greetings from Idle.

New St.

46   **THE GREEN** seen from Albion Road and **NEW STREET**. The upper photograph shows the chimney of Green Mill, and on the left part of the roof of the mill itself, remembered now for its final use as Idle Picture House. New Street was developed between 1875 and 1880; originally intended as a continuation of Apperley Road, the description "the new street" eventually

High Street

47 **BOTTOM OF HIGH STREET** with the offices of Walter Scott, coal merchant, formerly the White Horse Inn and now demolished to make a car and lorry bay for Watmoughs, the printing firm.

48 and 49 **JOHN GARNETT'S OFFICE** by the Railway Bridge, in two stages of development. Behind can be seen the old buildings of Watmoughs: their office off High Street still encases the original house.

Farms and Houses

50 CHURCH FARM
between Holy Trinity Church
and The Grange was
demolished to enlarge the
churchyard. This was one of
the older stone houses in
Idle, showing early 17th
century characteristics.
Those houses built of lesser
quality wallstones were
usually rendered – plastered
or painted over – as was the
case with this cottage.

51 **COTTAGES** at Burnwells. This small group of houses, built around an old public well, include many with three storeys and large windows to get the light, suggesting the inhabitants were weavers as well as small farmers. The photograph shows the Clapham family.

52 and 53 **BIRK HILL FARM**, near Park Road, Thackley.

54 **CROSS ROAD**, Simpson Green.
On the left are examples of the
suburban houses being built in Idle
during the late 19th and early 20th
centuries. They face the Recreation
Ground, and in the distance on the
right can be seen the buildings of
New Mill.

55 **PUMP** at Ashfield. Idle did not
get a suitable piped water system
until 1881, so pumps and wells
would have been essential for most
Idle inhabitants in the 19th century.

Buck Wood

56 **BUCK WOOD**.

These woods are on the rising ground in the curve of the River Aire that remains now the only part of the Township of Idle that has not been built on.

The woods take their name from the Buck family, who held the manorial water corn mill on the banks of the river for at least 200 years. All tenants of the Lord of the Manor were expected to take their corn to be ground only at this Mill, a practice that went on until the 18th century. The Bucks also developed a fulling mill, which continued as a textile mill into the 20th century.

Mills

57 **BUCK MILL** and **BRIDGE**.

The original crossing at this point on the river was by stepping stones. The need for a bridge to improve communication with Baildon was first voiced in 1873, but it was not built until 1889, as a joint venture between the Local Boards of Idle and Baildon.

The Mill has now been demolished and only a few foundations mark what had been an important centre of Idle life since medieval times.

Albion Mill is partly in Idle and partly in Eccleshill. Pighills Beck, which marks the boundary, fed the Mill pool, and now runs under the road at the Albion Road/Leeds Road junction. The photographs here show the dramatic fire in 1911. The mill was rebuilt, and is one of the few remaining mills in Idle.

58 **FIRE AT ALBION MILL**, 1911.

59 and 60 **AFTERMATH** of the fire at Albion Mill.

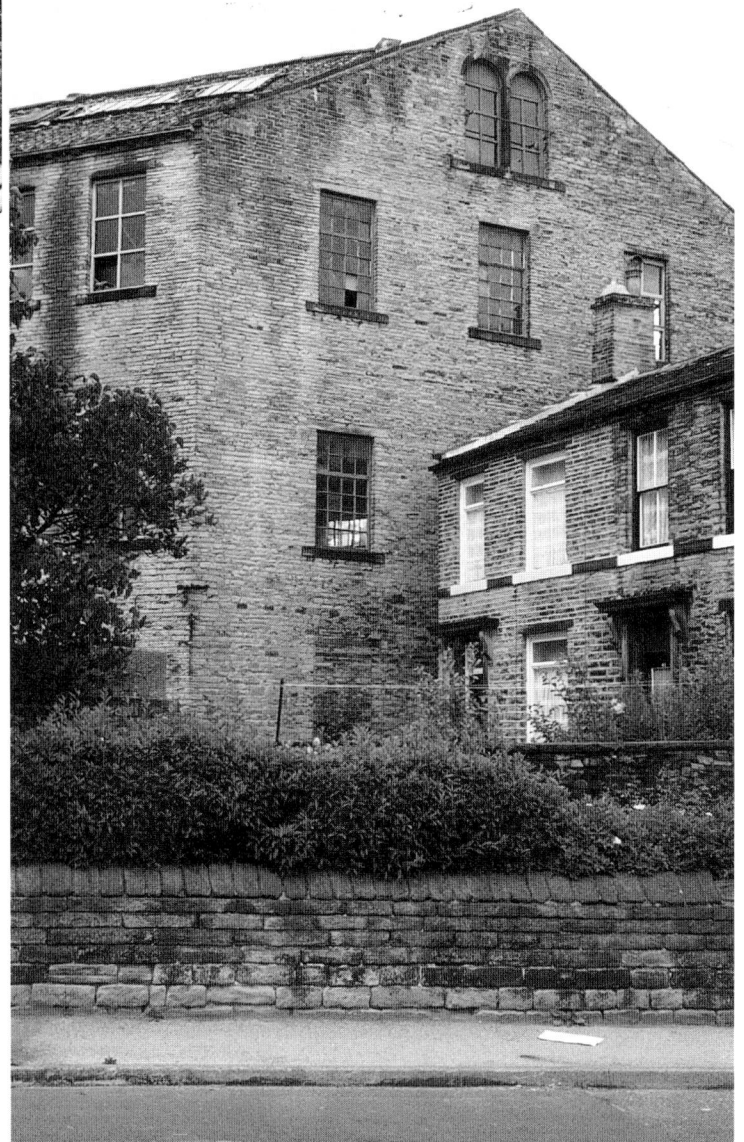

61 and 62 **NEW MILL**, Cross
Road, just before
demolition in 1993.

More Idle Folk

63 **IDLE FRIENDS**: sisters Ina Wright and Ida Suttle, Percy Baldwin,
Mr and Mrs Dawson with Henry and Helen, Bertha Beebee and a
visitor, outside a house in the Newkin at Hampton Place.

*Families and friends posed for their photographs against a background of
stone.*

64 **THE BOTTOMLEY FAMILY** in Back Lane behind the former
White Hart Inn (now the Spiritualist Church). The Bottomleys were a
family of butchers.
(Back row, left to right: John, Herbert, Kate, Ben and Dick;
Centre: Grandad, Alice, Annie and Grandma; Front: Louie).

65 **IDLE CONGRE-
GATIONAL ATHLETIC
CLUB**, seated between the
Sunday School building and
the mistal of Back Lane
Farm.

66   **PUPILS AT IDLE CHURCH SCHOOL.**
This building, just below the parish church, was demolished in 1974, to
allow for the expansion of Watmoughs printing firm.

67 **HAYMAKING** time at Back Lane Farm. Leonard Pearson as a boy
worked at the farm. The lettering on the prop reads "J. Hammond. 80
years 1908 success to the Farmers".

68 **HARVEST FESTIVAL DISPLAY** at Upper Chapel at the end of
the 1930s. The minister is John Gomer Williams.

*Until the middle of the 20th
century, Idle retained many
working farms, and Harvest
Festival was a relevant
celebration.*

69 **IDLE CRICKET CLUB**, c.1885.

ACKNOWLEDGEMENTS

Select Bibliography

The Bradford Antiquary Vol. I (1888)

William Cudworth, *Round About Bradford* (1876)

Holy Trinity, Idle 1830-1989 (Idle, 1989)

Milton Hudson, *The Bradford Canal* (Windhill Memories Group, 1996)

The Post Office Bradford Directory (1883)

Arthur Saul, *Idle Village: Old Settlement Area* (Bradford Metropolitan Council, Planning Division, 1977)

George Sheeran, *Good Houses Built of Stone* (Stanningley, Allanwood Books, 1986)

Thackley Methodist Church 1889-1989 (Thackley, 1989)

Wright Watson, *Idlethorp* (1950)

Original documents at the West Yorkshire Archive Service: Bradford include –

Idle Local Board Minute Books:

  BBT 8/1/2, p. 38 – naming of Leeds Road

  BBT 8/1/3, pp. 127, 131 and 147 – dis-turnpiked roads

  BBT 8/1/6 and 7, entries from 1887 to 1890 – Idle Local Board Offices and Buck Mill Bridge

DB/4/4/11 – Act for the Shipley to Bramley Turnpike Road

DB 4/4/23 – Act for making the Leeds and Liverpool Canal, 1770

Vints and Idle Quarrying:

  10 D 76/3/181/4 – Windhill Local Board v. Vint

  10 D 76/3/507 – Dawson v. Vint

  10 D 76/3/1137 – Vints als. Stead

10 D 76/4/21 – Boat traffic on the Leeds and Liverpool Canal, 1883

Sources of Photographs

John Barrett – 35; Kenneth Bottomley – 1, 4, 64; Emma Briggs – 13, 14, 15; Joe Brow – 63; Richard Eva – 53; Geoffrey Garnett – 8, 16, 17, 19, 20, 21, 22, 25, 26, 28, 29, 32, 39, 40, 41, 42 43, 44, 45, 47, 50, 56, 57, 59, 70; Mary Heggs – 18, 23, 54, 55; Ronnie Hudson – 31; Donald Jacks – 38; Gwyn Jude – 48, 49; Harry Jude – 36; Margaret King – 30; Clarice Marsay – 67; Mrs. Peirson – 69; Alex Robinson – 6, 52, 66; Derek Shepherd – 7; Mary Tidmarsh – 58, 60; Graham Townsend – 2, 9, 10, 11, 12; Jessie Waterhouse – 51; Eileen White – 61, 62; Wilfred White – 24, 68; Gladys Wright – 33, 34; Unattributed – 3, 5, 27, 37, 46, 65

My apologies to all those whose names I have omitted through ignorance or forgetfulness.   E.W.

I am grateful to these people for help in obtaining photographs and for information:

Stanley Ackroyd, The staff of the Bradford Archives, Geoffrey Garnett, Hilda Hepworth, Sheila Laycock, Thomas Mathers, Ernest Morris, Alice Nutter, Barbara Raistrick, Derek Shepherd, Emily Twedale, Martin White, Peter White, Windhill Memories Group, and members of the Idle and Thackley Heritage Group. Once again, the Idle and Thackley Heritage Group thanks John Barrett for his work on our publications.

Mary Heggs, 1934-1996

I would like to add a special appreciation of Mary, who provided several photographs used in all these books, and whose friendship, interest and information were a great help. She died after a courageous fight against cancer, and is missed by all who knew her.

The Idle and Thackley Heritage Group meets on the first Thursday of every month at 10.30a.m., and the third Wednesday of every month at 7.30p.m. at the Idle Baptist Church and Community Centre, Bradford Road, Idle, Bradford BD10 9PE.

70   **VIEW OF IDLE HILL** from near Brackendale Mill, Thackley; this semi-rural aspect of Idle has completely gone.